Level 5.5
Interest (MG 4-8)
0.5 pts.

Centipede

Karen Povey

KIDHAVEN PRESS™

THOMSON

™

GALE

San Diego • Detroit • New York • San Francisco • Cleveland
New Haven, Conn. • Waterville, Maine • London • Munich

THOMSON

GALE

LIBRARY OF CONGRESS CATALOGING-IN-PUBLICATION DATA

Povey, Karen D., 1962–
  Centipede / by Karen Povey.
    p. cm. — (Bugs)
Summary: Describes the physical characteristics, behavior, and habitat of centipedes.
  ISBN 0-7377-1766-1 (hardcover : alk. paper)
  1. Centipedes—Juvenile literature. [1. Centipedes.] I. Title. II. Series.
  QL449.5.P68 2004
  595 .6'2—dc22

                                                   2003015274

CONTENTS

Legs in Motion

Beneath the soil and rotting leaves that cover the forest floor lives a fierce hunter with a big appetite. That creature is the centipede. Centipedes are commonly found in forests all over the world, but they can live in many other places as well. Grasslands, deserts, caves, and gardens can all be homes to centipedes. One type of centipede, the house centipede, has even learned to live and hunt in people's homes.

Opposite: More than three thousand different types of centipedes are found throughout the world.

5

Most centipedes are one or two inches long, and yellow, or reddish brown in color.

Altogether, there are more than three thousand different kinds of centipedes. Most are very small, measuring just an inch or two in length. Others, especially those that live in warm parts of the world, are much larger. The Peruvian giant centipede from the South American rain forest can grow up to twelve inches long.

A Rainbow of Colors

Most centipedes are yellow, brown, or reddish brown. However, some of the larger species found in deserts or tropical forests are decorated with bright, beautiful colors. These giant centipedes of Asia, Africa, or South America may appear in a variety of bold colors including jet-black, brilliant blue, fire red, and bright orange.

Centipede Structure

Centipedes may be different in color or size, but otherwise they are all very much alike. Centipedes are members of the **arthropod** family, the largest group of animals on the earth. Centipedes, like all arthropods, have a hard shell-like covering, called the **exoskeleton**. The exoskeleton is on the outside of the centipede's body. It acts like a suit of armor to protect the centipede.

Centipedes have bodies that are divided into two sections. The first section is the head, which contains the centipede's **antennae** and mouth. The second section is the main part of the body, called the **trunk**. The trunk is made up of many small **segments**, each with one pair of jointed legs attached to it.

Fancy Footwork

Centipedes have from 30 to 350 legs, depending on the species. With that many legs, how do centipedes move so quickly without tripping? The secret lies in several special features. First, the centipede's segments are connected by flexible tissue. As the centipede runs, the segments stretch apart, making the distance between the legs grow longer. Second, each pair of legs is a little longer than the pair in front of it. This difference in leg length keeps the centipede from stepping on itself. Finally, the legs

The centipede's body is made up of many segments, each with a pair of legs attached to it.

1 Two antennae detect smells, heat, and movement, and help the centipede track down prey. Sharp jawlike claws called prehensors attack prey and inject deadly poison, or venom, into the centipede's victim.

3 Strong, shell-like covering, or exoskeleton, protects the centipede's soft insides.

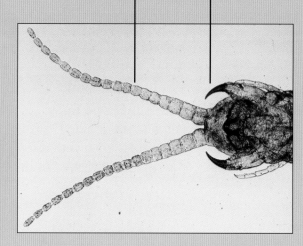

2 Segmented body is able to twist and turn in many directions. Each segment has one pair of legs.

move together in a special rhythm. Movement begins closest to the head and continues backward in a wavelike motion. With this arrangement, when the centipede moves forward only a few of its feet touch the ground at any time.

A Fast Runner

The fastest centipedes can speed along, traveling twenty inches every second. Zipping along on so many legs requires centipedes to pump lots of oxygen to their hardworking muscles. Centipedes do not breathe through lungs. Instead, air moves directly to body tissues through holes, called spiracles, at the base of the legs.

As they run, tiny claws on the centipede's feet help it to grip the ground. Claws also help a centipede cling to steep surfaces. The house centipede can use its claws to climb straight up a wall!

Most of the time, though, centipedes stay hidden from view. But these amazing creatures reward observers interested in taking a closer look into their private, fascinating lives.

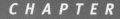

CHAPTER

A Secret Life

Opposite: Centipedes spend most of their lives alone, hidden out of sight.

Centipedes spend most of their lives alone. When it is time to breed, however, male and female centipedes must get together. Because centipedes usually stay hidden, finding a mate can be difficult. To attract a male, the female gives off a special scent called a **pheromone**. The male centipede smells the pheromone by waving his antennae through the air, capturing the scent. He follows the trail of scent until he finds the female's hiding place.

Centipede Breeding

With some types of centipedes, males and females begin mating by touching each other while turning together in a circle. After this courtship "dance," the centipedes will breed. To breed, the male centipede will first spin a small web of silk. Next, he will deposit his sperm onto the web. The sperm is in a sealed packet called a **spermatophore**. The male will use his legs to guide the female over the spermatophore. Once the female is in the correct position, she will use a special pair of legs, called **claspers**, to lift the spermatophore and bring the sperm into her body.

A Safe Nest

After breeding, the female centipede must find a safe place to lay her eggs. Damp soil or rotten wood provides a perfect environment for the eggs to develop. Some centipedes dig holes for their eggs. The female will lay just one egg in each hole. Afterwards, she will cover each egg with soil and leave it.

Other centipedes are more watchful mothers. The large centipedes that live in South America lay up to

A female centipede protects her eggs (above). The female guards her young (right) until they are strong enough to leave the nest.

Each segment of the centipede's body (above) has one pair of legs. At right, a centipede uses its many legs to climb a blade of grass.

sixty eggs in a simple nest of wood or soil. These centipedes stay with their eggs, curling around them to protect them from harm. As she guards the eggs, the centipede cleans them with her mouth. This prevents harmful fungus from growing on the eggs and killing the young developing inside. She also tries to protect the eggs from predators. When the young hatch, the female guards them until they are strong enough to leave the nest. The mother centipede may spend up to two months looking after her eggs and young. During this time she never leaves, not even to eat or drink.

Gaining Legs

Newly hatched centipedes, called **larvae**, usually have fewer pairs of legs than the adults. A house-centipede larva, for example, has only four pairs of legs when it hatches. As it grows, the larva sheds its exoskeleton in exchange for a larger one that takes its place. This process is called **molting**. Each time the larva molts, it gains additional pairs of legs. The house-centipede larva molts five times before it has fifteen pairs of legs, the same number as the adults.

Centipedes may take up to three years to become adults that are able to breed. Compared to many other arthropods, centipedes live a long time. Some species are known to live up to six years. To live this long, each centipede must stay safe by finding the perfect place to make its home.

Hidden Homes

Centipedes like to stay out of sight. Any dark, hidden spot, even a small one, can be a safe home for a centipede. Centipedes can squeeze between rocks, scurry beneath logs, and wriggle through the soil. The centipede is well suited for life in these tight places. Centipedes have bodies that are very flat and thin. This shape allows a centipede to slide easily into narrow cracks between rocks or under the bark of a tree.

The centipede's shape also allows it to move very fast. If a centipede is discovered in its home, it will quickly dart away to find a new hiding spot. Most centipedes have colors that match the leaves and soil, helping them to hide. This coloring, called **camouflage**, allows them to blend into the background so they cannot be seen easily.

This centipede's color disguises it among the leaves and soil.

Keeping Its Cool

For a centipede, staying underground or buried in leaves is important for staying alive. A centipede can lose water through the spiracles on its body. It can also lose water through its exoskeleton. By staying where it is cool and damp, a centipede can avoid losing too much water and drying out.

Another way centipedes stay moist is by being **nocturnal**. They rest in their hiding spots during the day and move about hunting at night when it is usually cooler and damper.

Desert Life

Being nocturnal is especially important for desert centipedes that live in the American Southwest. The hot desert sun would quickly dry out and kill a centipede that ventured out during the day. Instead, desert centipedes spend the day under rocks or hiding in the burrows of other animals. During the hottest part of the summer, desert centipedes might stay hidden all night, too. But if a summer rain shower begins, the centipede will dash out of its hole

Desert centipedes (above) hide under rocks during the day (left) and come out at night to hunt.

to hunt and explore while the desert is cool and wet.

At Home in a Cave

Cave centipedes do not have to worry about drying out. The caves in which these centipedes live are cool and damp both day and night, all year long. Therefore, cave centipedes

This burrowing centipede lives in damp soil and under rocks, safe from predators and the heat of the sun.

can be active at any time. The darkness of the cave provides the protection this shy creature needs. As it hunts in the dark, a cave centipede scurries around on the moist cave floor or creeps up the cave walls.

Seashore Centipedes

Some other types of centipedes also make their homes where staying damp is no problem. Marine centipedes live on ocean beaches. They hide under

Like all centipedes, the Peruvian giant centipede spends the day hiding in dark places and hunts at night.

stones or seaweed. Sometimes they move into empty barnacle shells. These seashore centipedes always live close to the waves so their homes will stay wet.

Although they live in many different places, all centipedes share the same secretive habits. But when they emerge from their homes to hunt, these shy centipedes become fearsome predators.

Fierce Hunters

Centipedes are some of the fiercest hunters in the bug world. The smallest centipedes, such as the house centipede, will hunt small prey. They find insects, spiders, and worms for their meals. Larger centipedes, however, can tackle larger prey such as snails, slugs, and lizards. The giant centipedes that live in tropical forests are fierce predators. They will eat animals that are almost as large as they are! The Puerto

Rican giant centipede, for example, will eat frogs, small mice, and even baby rats.

Super Sensors

Many types of centipedes have poor eyesight or no eyes at all. Instead of eyes, a pair of antennae gives the centipede the information it needs for hunting. The sensitive antennae can detect smells, movement, and heat. A centipede will use its antennae to track down its prey. By waving them through the air, a centipede

The centipede uses its antennae to track down prey. Here, a centipede has been magnified thirty times.

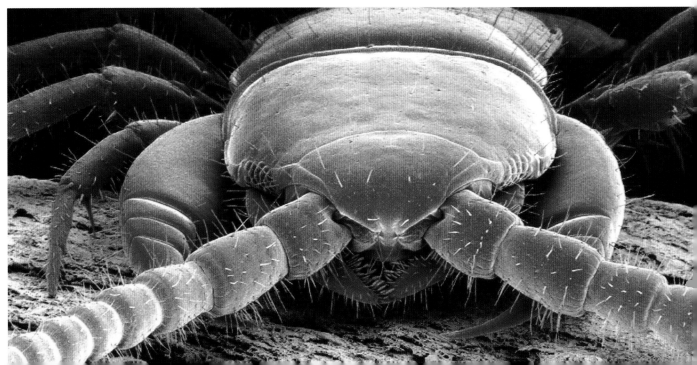

With a firm grip on a caterpillar, a centipede injects venom to quickly kill its prey.

can follow the scent trail of a potential meal. The antennae can also feel vibrations on the ground as other animals approach.

A Deadly Bite

Once prey is found, the centipede will grab it tightly with the first pair of legs below its head. These legs, called **prehensors**, act like jaws to catch and kill prey. The ends of the prehensors have sharp, fanglike claws. These claws are connected to **venom** glands in the centipede's body. The centipede will pump powerful venom through the claws into its victim, killing it quickly.

The venom will begin to dissolve the body tissues of the prey, making it easy for the centipede to feed. A centipede will eat by chewing the softened prey with two pairs of jaws on the underside of its head.

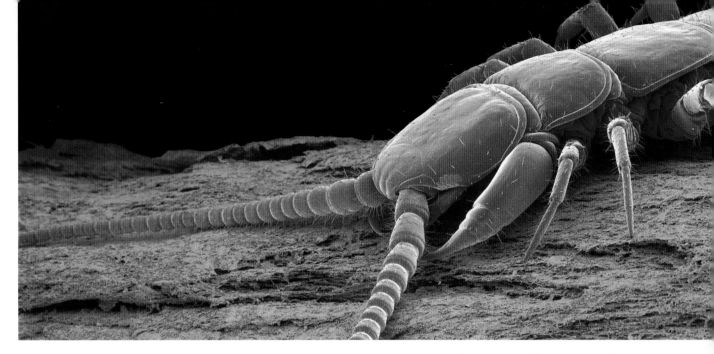

Staying Safe

Although the centipede is an aggressive hunter, it must sometimes protect itself. Larger predators, such as birds, shrews, and toads, may try to eat centipedes. Centipedes have several different ways they can defend themselves. Some centipedes have special glands that can produce a sticky, smelly liquid. This liquid may drive away the predator. Or, the liquid may stick to a predator. Trapped by the sticky substance, the

The centipede uses its claws and venomous bite to ward off predators.

predator cannot attack. Some centipedes can purposely drop off legs to distract a predator when it attacks. The fallen legs will continue to twitch while the centipede scurries off to hide. Centipedes can also use their prickly hind legs to pinch their enemies.

The centipede's most powerful defense, however, is its bite. Even a small centipede's venom is strong enough to be very painful, even to people. A bite from a giant centipede can cause severe swelling, headaches, and a racing heartbeat in humans. Because they are so dangerous, giant centipedes do not have to stay hidden as much as the smaller centipedes do. The giant centipedes' bright colors act as a warning to predators that they are dangerous and are not safe to attack.

Fortunately, centipedes are not aggressive toward people unless they are provoked. Instead, they spend their time quietly hunting and hiding as they go about their secret lives.

GLOSSARY

antennae: The feelers on a centipede's head used for smelling and detecting movement or heat.

arthropod: The large scientific grouping of animals that includes centipedes.

camouflage: The ability to blend into the surrounding environment to hide from predators or prey.

claspers: A specialized pair of legs a female centipede uses for picking up the male's sperm while breeding.

exoskeleton: The hard, shell-like outer covering of a centipede's body.

larva (plural—larvae): A young centipede.

molt: The shedding of its exoskeleton as the centipede grows.

nocturnal: Active at night.

pheromones: Chemical signals released by a female centipede to attract a mate.

prehensors: The centipede's first pair of legs, used for grabbing prey.

segments: The parts that make up a centipede's trunk, each with a pair of legs attached.

spermatophore: A sealed packet that contains the male centipede's sperm.

spiracles: Holes near the base of the centipede's legs that are used for taking in air.

trunk: The main part of a centipede's body.

venom: A poisonous fluid used by a centipede to kill its prey.

FOR FURTHER EXPLORATION

Books

Jason Cooper, *Centipedes.* Vero Beach, FL: Rourke, 1996. A simple introduction to the lives and habits of centipedes.

Theresa Greenway, *Mini Pets: Centipedes and Millipedes.* Austin, TX: Raintree Steck-Vaughn, 2000. This book describes how to find and observe centipedes in the forest or garden.

Frank Lowenstein and Sheryl Lechner, *Bugs: Insects, Spiders, Centipedes, Millipedes and Other Closely Related Arthropods.* Black Dog and Leventhal, 1999. Detailed information on arthropods including full-color, close-up photographs of animals in their natural habitats.

Christopher O'Toole, ed., *Firefly Encyclopedia of Insects and Spiders.* Toronto: Firefly Books, 2002. A complete look at the biology and behavior of arthropods, including centipedes.

Websites

Backyard Nature (www.backyard nature.net/2arthrop.htm). Natural history writer Jim Conrad has created a website filled with information on centipedes and other related arthropods.

University of Kentucky Department of Entomology (www. uky.edu/Agriculture/CritterFiles/ casefile/relatives/relatives.htm). This website contains photos, facts, descriptions, and myths about centipedes and other arthropods.

INDEX

PICTURE CREDITS

ABOUT THE AUTHOR

Karen Povey received her bachelor's degree in zoology at the University of California, Davis, and her master's degree in education at the University of Washington. She has spent her career as a conservation educator, working to instill in people of all ages an appreciation for wildlife. Karen makes her home in Washington where she manages and presents live-animal education programs at Tacoma's Point Defiance Zoo & Aquarium. Karen enjoys traveling with her husband and spending time with her dogs and horses.